BEATING THE BARRIERS

THE CODE OF LIFE

OSHIN ARORA

Copyright © Oshin Arora
All Rights Reserved.

This book has been published with all efforts taken to make the material error-free after the consent of the author. However, the author and the publisher do not assume and hereby disclaim any liability to any party for any loss, damage, or disruption caused by errors or omissions, whether such errors or omissions result from negligence, accident, or any other cause.

While every effort has been made to avoid any mistake or omission, this publication is being sold on the condition and understanding that neither the author nor the publishers or printers would be liable in any manner to any person by reason of any mistake or omission in this publication or for any action taken or omitted to be taken or advice rendered or accepted on the basis of this work. For any defect in printing or binding the publishers will be liable only to replace the defective copy by another copy of this work then available.

Writing is a long journey where you need both- some inspiration and some motivation. to make my journey fruitful and daring, the dedications goes to- My parents, My hardwork, My aim, My spirit and ofcourse in what case can I forget NotionPress? A huge gratitude to Notionpress who actually supported me to fulfil my aims and hereby all my gratitude goes to the above mentioned. Well, some mentions may seem strange, but dedication can be anything and everything, and not only a living person.

Contents

Contents

Preface

Do you believe you can never get successful? Do you really? So believe in your luck as you purchased this book! This book will create wonders in your journey to become successful and wealthy by giving you advises to beat the barriers that makes a red light for you! I chose to write on this topic as many people now-a-days should self-help them but instead they just dream and believes that some miracle will happen to reach them to thier goals. But just within a snap, the whole life can change! This is how just by reading this novella your journey would take a turn! All the young people who wants to achieve their aims in life became my motivation and inspiration. Though, it was a long proccess to research on such a delicate topic but ya, it was a journey where I realised that it's not that easy to reach the building of your goals! It took me around 6 months to complete this project of mine! Well, I would be glad to help you through this book!

ONE
SUCCESS

Starting with a sensitive and a broad topic!

There are many definitions, but there's one thing all the greats agree on: Success only comes by persevering despite failure. You become successful when you achieve your goal(s) not when you start earning lakhs or crores/ millions. Success provides confidence, security, a sense of well-being, the ability to contribute at a greater level, hope and leadership. Without success, you, the group, your company, your goals, dreams and even entire civilizations cease to survive. Success should never be reduced to something that does not matter or isn't important. It is vital and should be held as such! Regardless of what goals you are trying to attain, success is important. Quit succeeding, and you quit winning; quit winning long enough, and you will quit! Success doesn't come easy, and one must understand while setting on the journey. This book will tell you some easy-to-use and easy-to-understand ideas that would help you to be successful in life ahead. This will make you count some of your mistakes that you'll might do in the journey towards the success. To achieve success, one has to be persistent, focused, be focused and work diligently towards achieving their goal. When you believe you are lacking behind, you can go through the list in this book to be motivated. This book will give you some quick tips that will avoid all the faults you may make in the journey. It's always advisable to avoid faults but they are too necessary! But how? Read ahead!

Focus and Distractions

'Your focus determines your reality' — Jedi Knight Qui-Gon Jinn

Almost 60% people when asked what stops them for being successful, they answer 'Distraction'. Well just assume that you and 'Distraction' will have a wrestling competition and Distraction will use the technique of distracting you but what will you use as a weakness for distraction? 'Focus', when you focus no one can distract you but you have to remember that focus is as a naughty kid who won't come itself, you have to bring it and handle it by having control on yourself. When you know you have to focus it seems difficult but when you don't realise that you are actually focusing, it becomes easy! That's true even if sounds no sense and this is the human nature. Just Imagine that I give you 6 balls in your hands and I instruct you to distribute it among 6 people but make sure no ball falls, you will not be even knowing that what person was doing while you were distributing the balls because you were focusing and even you can try it! Some good ways to be focused are meditation, yoga and exercising. Highly successful people create a to-do list the night before, focusing on their most important tasks (MITs). They go on to break down those tasks into smaller, easier-accomplished subtasks. Each hour of the day is planned so that they don't tend to become distracted and lose track of the original tasks at hand. Focus is so important because it is the gateway to all thinking: perception, memory, learning, reasoning, problem solving, and decision making. Without good focus, all aspects of your ability to think will suffer.

Experience

'Never regret. If it's good, it's wonderful. If it's bad, it's experience' —
Victoria Holt

Many people underestimate themselves by giving the excuse 'I am not
experienced'. When you started walking first time, were you experienced?
When you started talking first time, were you experienced? Of course no,
right? When you don't start doing anything, you can't be 'Experienced'. Just
assume that I instruct you to write a book, you'll say I don't know because
I am not experienced. If I'll tell you to do a totally new experiment you will
refuse because you aren't experienced. Was I experienced when I wrote my
first book or was Albert Einstein experienced when he discovered the
theory of relativity? No. But still we all succeed in the task we start. Hence,
don't make limitations on yourself on the basis of 'Experience'. There are
people who don't make a lot of mistakes and just learn the basics right and
become successful without actually having to experience it all.

Age

'How old would you be if you don't know how old you are?'

Age is nothing but a simple number but you limit yourself based on this normal number. When you feel to take a step ahead in life, you limit yourself that no, either you are too early or too late and this is the reason you never become successful. So irrespective of age, you will have your 'own' reasons to do it, love it, embrace it, no matter what people say. Maybe that 'love' makes you ageless and maybe age is just a mere thought to show its value. Age is nothing but a three letter word, to which we have attached great significance. Somehow, we have given more meaning than we should, and so we let a number to control our life. The truth is that age does not define us, or our destiny, because it is not our age that counts, but our attitude and will. Those who dare to become their truest version will find a deeper purpose in life. And, when life has a purpose, time has no boundaries. When time has no boundaries, age really is just a number! I feel it's important to dispel the myth that age can signify, 'too early' or 'too late'; as plenty can still be achieved, what ever your age. Age never stops a person from getting successful but it's your mind who does that. So defeat your mind and show it, that it's the right time to get what you want.

Procrastination

'Procrastination is the thief of time'!

It is a known fact that we all tend to postpone matters, we are indecisive and given a choice we would like others to be doing work and we simply enjoying a cool time. When it comes to us, we try to get away by saying, "Very busy, no time." Don't we? Procrastination is as a credit card, it's a lot of until you get the bill. Procrastination is the action of unnecessarily and voluntarily delaying or postponing something despite knowing that there will be negative consequences for doing so. The main reason people doesn't become successful is 'Procrastination'. The very famous Hindi Doha also represents this, 'Kal kare so aaj, aaj kare so ab' by Rahim Das. This represents that the work you delayed for tomorrow should be done today and infact, now! Procrastination diverts time away from important or necessary tasks, and spends it on less important activities. The end result is you have less time to do what is really important. With less time to complete assessment tasks, the accuracy of your work and quality of the content are likely to suffer. A very successful person Thomas C. Corley, avoided the costly habit of procrastination. But how to cure the issue of Procrastination? Here are few advices:

- Set Deadlines (If not adhered, then punishments)

- Don't find a particular alternative

- Remove Distraction word from your dictionary

- Make a strict schedule.

Having Unlike Thoughts

'If everyone thinks alike, then no one is thinking' — George S. Patton

Today's people especially today's generation underestimate themselves on having 'Unlike thoughts'. Let's have a situation! There was an event going on and Sam and Ellen were called on the stage to share their future plans. Sam wanted to become a doctor and at the other hand, Ellen wanted to become an engineer. As they both had unlike thoughts, Sam's mind stroked with a thought of 'Having Unlike Thoughts' issue. He thought that if Ellen wants to be an engineer then engineer would be a better profession than a doctor. This mere thought, actually destroyed a good life of Sam. If we get out of this mind-set, you'll find that both the professions are equally essential as without doctor there is no life and without an engineer, there are no roads and buildings. Having Unlike Thoughts doesn't matter if you have a good goal in choice. Taking opinions is a different perspective here, but following it blindly and hiding your goals under it isn't a suitable idea. Therefore, having unlike thoughts is just a mere thought!

Fear of Failure

'It's not failure that holds you back, it's the fear of failure that paralyzes you' — Brian Tracy

We can find this mere thought called 'Fear of Failure' in almost every person present on the Earth. The fear of failure, which is sometimes referred to as atychiphobia , is an irrational and persistent fear of failing. Sometimes this fear might emerge in response to a specific situation. Even before you start, you get this phobia of getting failed. Do you know that Thomas Edison failed 1000 times before inventing the blub? If he would had gave up, you won't had that small bulb to switch on at night. We all have different definitions of failure, simply because we all have different benchmarks, values, and belief systems. A failure to one person might simply be a great learning experience for someone else. It's important to realize that in everything we do, there's always a chance that we'll fail. Facing that chance, and embracing it, is not only courageous – it also gives us a fuller, more rewarding life. If you can't overcome this phobia, analyse that you can never be successful. Follow these ways to overcome it:

• No Shame Policy: When Rita stood at her bench to answer a question, everyone laughed hard at her because the answer was extremely non-sense. This attracted her to the 'Fear of Failure'. Make sure, you have an environment with No Shame Policy and even if you experience it, the best way is to talk to your parents about it.

• Forget the mistake, Remember the lesson: You get fail because of a mistake. However, when you point that mistake out and fix it and try again, you'll experience 'Success'. So you have to forget the mistake and remember the lesson so that the mistake isn't repeated.

• Focus on learning: The chips aren't always going to fall where you want them to — but if you understand that reality going in, you can be prepared to wring the most value out of the experience, no matter the outcome.

So now come out of this phobia if want to be successful.

Ignorance

'Where ignorance is our master, there is no possibility of peace'— Dalai Lama

The world is continuously changing, if you refuse to learn, you will be outdated. Knowledge is power. Learning doesn't end in school. Whatever field you are in, you need to learn and update yourself with information constantly. Successful people have a habit of learning. If you find yourself constantly failing at something, don't convince yourself success is on the way. No! Genuinely ask yourself whether your failures are not self-inflicted as a result of your ignorance. If you want to open a coffee shop, but know nothing about coffee, no amount of determination and persistence will make you successful at it. Gaining knowledge is the most essential stepping stone to success and infact, it's the 1st (or maybe 2nd but no later than that) stepping stone to success. Persistently approaching your dreams in ignorance will persistently give you failure and defeat as results. Find time and learn first. Whatever you want to endeavour in, spend 90% of your time learning about it. Do not do anything without first learning, do not go into a business you do not fully understand.

Lack of Self-Believe

'Believe you can, and you're almost there' — Theodore Roosevelt

What is self-believing? Self-believe is something that controls 50% of your life even if you don't know. Self-believing can be the biggest motivation for you as time flies. Believing in yourself helps you to be energetic and a person who never gives up. It will also build an ability to focus. Chances are your negative sense of who you are is either outdated or simply untrue, and has been passed to you from others such as your parents, colleagues, etc. Try telling yourself that you are a good person and you are worthy of love and respect just like everyone else. Don't be afraid to rewrite your own script – it's your life. People believe what you tell them, so if you project failure and inadequacy your friends and colleagues might start to agree. Practise projecting yourself as someone whose opinions are just as valid as others, and your sense of self-worth will begin to rise. If you build Self-believe in yourself it will definitely help you to be successful. Let's have a story on it! Payal used to always de-motivate her when she used to start-up something. Before she gave exam of IIT, she had a mere thought 'I'll not be able do it'. However, she cleared it. In second exam also she had this thought. She wasn't able to clear the second exam and hence, as she de-motivated herself, she didn't studied as she already predicted her future. If she had not predicted herself and studied, it would helped her with a hope of clearing the exam. Therefore, your motivation for you is the most essential part.

Too many Expectations

'Don't blame people for disappointing you, blame yourself for expecting too much' — Mary Louisa Molesworth

No here and there talks, directly coming on the point. Having too many expectations can unexpectedly ruin your path of success. When you have too many expectations, even any 1 of them isn't fulfilled, your self confidence would be broken and there will be a 'Fear of Failure' glowed in you. As a human being, you can't achieve all your expectations. But what you have achieved, work on that and make it more powerful. The tricky thing about your expectations is that they impact other people too. As far back as the 1960s, Harvard research demonstrated the power of our beliefs in swaying other people's behaviour. When teachers in the studies were told that certain (randomly selected) children were smart, those kids performed better, not only in the classroom, but also on standardized IQ tests. One of the most important things a person can do is stick his or her neck out and seek opportunity. Just because you deserve a raise, a promotion, or a company car, doesn't mean it's going to happen. You have to make it happen. You have to put in the hard work, then go and get what's yours. If we limit ourselves to what's given to us, we are at the mercy of other people. When you take action, think "what steps do I need to take?" "what obstacles are in my way and what do I need to do to remove them?" and "what mistakes am I making that take me away from my goals rather than toward them?" Let's have a story for this as well! Kiara always had high expectations. She gave the exam of UPSC which she was able to crack. She wanted to become a Magistrate (Judge) but her expectations went unexpected as she got the position in IPS, though it was a good opportunity but she didn't accepted it due to her expectations. Generally, people miss better opportunities for their future due to their high expectations.

Perfectionism

'Perfectionism is self-abuse of the highest order' — Anne Wilson Schaef

When we strive to be perfect, we set unrealistic and punishingly high standards, setting ourselves up for an all-or-nothing mentality. "I'm either successful or a failure." A study published in the Harvard Business Review found that perfectionism leads to increased levels of anxiety, burnout, and stress. A human being can never be perfect. There must be a talent in you as well (even if it is common). Don't let perfectionism control your barrier for success. A story for this as well- Cristina had dreamt to be 'The Most Successful' person in her life. Cristina wanted to be A doctor, an engineer and a scientist. She didn't understood that being perfect isn't possible yet for a person. As the result, she got failed in every field. If she had focused on one call, she would definitely had been successful. I believe many of us are perfectionists in our own right. We set high bars for ourselves and put our best foot forward to achieve them. We dedicate copious amounts of attention and time to our work to maintain our high personal standards. Our passion for excellence drives us to run the extra mile, never stopping, never relenting. Dedication towards perfection undoubtedly helps us to achieve great results. Yet, there is a hidden flip side to being perfectionists that we may not be aware of. Sure, being a perfectionist and having a keen eye for details help us improve and reach our goals. However, as ironic as it might sound, a high level of perfectionism prevents us from being our best as we begin to set unrealistic standards and let the fear of failure hold us back. As the above story also resulted in failure. Why perfectionism isn't so perfect?

- Less efficiency

- Less effectiveness

- Missing the bigger picture

The problem isn't perfectionism specifically. Perfectionism helps us to continuously strive for excellence and become better, so it can really be a good thing. The problem is when setting high standards turns into an obsession, so much so that the perfectionist becomes neurotic over gaining "perfection" and refuses to accept anything less than perfect. In the process, she/he misses the whole point altogether and does damage to their mental health. To overcome this phobia, use the 80/20 rule, where 80% of output can be achieved in 20% of time spent. We can spend all our time getting the 100% in, or we can draw the line where we get majority of the output, and start on a new project. Obsessing over details is draining and tedious, and it doesn't help us accomplish much. I used to review a blog post 3-4 times before I published. All the reviewing only amounted to subtle changes in phrasing and the occasional typos. It was extremely ineffective, so now I scan it once or twice and publish it.

Focusing on Outcomes only

'The journey not the arrival matters' — TS Eliot

It is easy to think that what you need to attain extraordinary success is to focus on results and use these results to measure your progress. However such application of a principle is far from optimal. There is more to success than just looking at results without understanding that at the end of the day it comes down to your consistency and the process involved in getting the job done. When you start focusing your attention and energy less on the results but rather on the processes or the techniques involved you discover that you learn faster, are more successful and even happier at the outcome. Altogether you gain more in life when you focus on the process rather than the results. When you start focusing your attention and energy less on the results but rather on the processes or the techniques involved you discover that you learn faster, are more successful and even happier at the outcome. Altogether you gain more in life when you focus on the process rather than the results. Mistakes are part of existence as no one is perfect. Mistakes help you learn and grow in life. When you are focused on a specific desired result you are less willing to experiment or take risks that may just propel you to a better outcome than the one you were actually aiming for. Success is a journey rather than a destination. When you are focused on the process you really are excited about being in the present and enjoying it more fully. You are engaged and you want to dig deep at those opportunities and avenues you can, because at the end of the day it becomes about learning faster and gaining experience.

Negative Attitude

'Bad attitude is like a flat tire, you'll never go anywhere until you change it'

Not only does negative thinking make it harder for you to think logically, but the fear of failure that is often associated with negativity slows down activity in the cerebellum. This results in a reduced ability to come up with creative solutions to the problems you face. Let's have a story for this as well. Sophia's goal was becoming an IPS Officer. But, as everything needs hardwork, the same was needed to fulfil her goal. It was actually a blessing in disguise as she was preparing for the exam. But her mind was full of negative thoughts such as- I'll not be able to clear the exam, it's not the right way to study, it's not the right time to give the exam, I am not experienced, etc. In these thoughts, she just had to remove the word 'no' and then perceive the magic! If we'll throw out the negative thoughts, we'll be able to achieve anything we want. But how to give up negative thoughts? Here are few advices:

• Meditation helps relaxing and freshens your mind.

• Practice coping with criticisms.

• Identify your negative thoughts and replace them.

• Write it on a sheet, crumble it and throw (it's scientifically proved that this can help levelling negative thoughts).

• Establish and adapt a good-planned routine.

• Have a stress free environment.

• Put on Music.

• Take a walk in a big ground (preferably also jog).

• Practice self care.

• Wake up early morning (it helps to increase your life as well as your day).

Don't know what to do

'Find your goals within'

There are several personalities who had decided their future beforehand which is why they become successful. It's truly very logical that if you don't know what to do, you can't do! But what to do we don't know so we really have goals or not? If you start setting goals, that's OK. There are no mistakes on this journey — it's just a learning experience. If you live without goals and end up failing, ask yourself if it's really a failure. You only fail if you don't get to where you wanted to go — but if you don't have a destination in mind, there's no failure.

Analysis Paralysis

'Analysis is the critical starting point of strategic thinking' — Kenichi Ohmae

Many people let questions and doubts paralyze them. They believe they can't start on a goal until they have all the answers to every "what if" scenario. However, no matter how long and hard you prepare, you will never have all the answers to the questions you ask.
Additionally, most people make their decisions and/or answer their questions based on where they are right now, rather than on where they want to go or who they want to become. Always base your decisions and answer your questions with a view to the future, not a view to current situations. Your situation will change because of the decisions you make today and will dictate the success of your journey. So, move forward toward your goal knowing that you'll never have all the answers.

Complaining

‘Champions never complain, they are busy getting better’ — John Wooden

One of the main reason behind getting failure is complaining. Complaining is a next barrier for success. I can help you about this. Package a complaint as a sandwich. "Woe is me" has never won any friends. But positivity brings out the best in those around you. The complaint sandwich starts with a positive statement, followed by the complaint, and then closes with another positive statement. Here's an example: "I've heard great things about your service and I'm excited to try it. But I've had a difficult time reaching my account manager for immediate solutions. I'd really like to continue using your services. Is there anything you can do to help?" Structuring your complaints this way also helps the listener better understand where you're coming from. Take control and find more than one solution. You'll start moving in a different direction and take yourself from "helpless and hopeless" to "helpful and happier." Even if it's ultimately not the right answer, it will help create positive momentum. All the extra cortisol released by frequent complaining impairs your immune system and makes you more susceptible to high cholesterol, diabetes, heart disease, and obesity. It even makes the brain more vulnerable to strokes. Nothing shoots down a group discussion faster than the word "but." When one person floats an idea and another jumps in with "but," what comes next is always negative. And it invariably leads to disagreement. To improve team effectiveness, start replacing "but" with "and": "That's an interesting idea, and you might also consider". Let's have a story on it! John always used to complain. Whenever he used to be closer to the success and something would be changed due to less efficiency of hardwork, he used to complain about the situation and not blamed himself. Hence, he never got successful as a result. So you don't have to be complainer to be a successful person.

Maximizing your Goals

'You live and you learn' — Meshia

Some people have too many goals and not enough focus. It's like they're standing in front of a dart board with three targets in mind. Hitting just one target is difficult enough; hitting three targets simultaneously with one dart is impossible. Therefore, determine the one goal you are focused on and move forward with that one goal only. Eliminate other goals that are secondary. This is not to say that you should never have more than one goal. Rather, you need to realize that you have only so much time and energy. Therefore, choose the goal that will give you the highest ROE (return on effort) and focus on that one goal first. Once complete, you can then focus on other goals in sequence. Hence, minimize your goals and maximise your efforts. Let's have a story on this as well! Karuna had an archery competition in her school. The judging criteria was maximum shots in minimum time. Karuna decided to hit 2 goals together with both the hands as it would take less time and even increase the number of shots. What happened was not even a single shot was hitted by her on the dart which lead to her failure in the competition. This was because her brain wasn't able to focus on both hands together which lead to no focus in either hand also. Hence, if she would had minimized her goal to one-by-one shot, she would have had 90% of chances of winning. This clearly depicts that maximum goals = less efforts = no success and minimum goals = more efforts = success.

Negative Mentorship

'A mentor is someone who allows you to see the hope inside you' — Oprah Winfrey

Mentorship is something which is very important. But what about negative mentorship? This study addresses how perceived mentor and protégé values affect negative mentoring, organizational commitment, job satisfaction, and perceived career success. Results indicate that protégés with mentors perceived to have self-enhancement values experienced more negative mentoring while protégés with mentors perceived to have self-transcendence values experienced less negative mentoring. Those who experienced negative mentoring had less organizational commitment, job satisfaction and perceived career success. It was also found that negative mentoring indirectly mediated between perceived mentor values and the protégé outcomes (job satisfaction, organizational commitment, and perceived career success). Negative mentoring can leave more severe and lasting effects than positive ones. Hence, finding a good mentor is a need.

Not Risking

'If you don't risk anything, you risk even more' — Erica Jong

Taking risks eliminates the possibility of looking back and asking, "what if?" Even if you fail, you'll walk away with more experience and more knowledge, which can lead you to further success in other areas and at least one study shows that risk takers end up more satisfied with their lives because of it. Not risking is basically not trying. When you don't try, you can't even set aa goal so accomplishing it, is a far way thought. Indeed, risking is much harder than not trying but you can only achieve when you do hardwork. Hardwork isn't all about just waking up tonight and managing your goals, it's also about risking what you want to manage. Yet not taking risks in life for fear of discomfort and change often produces a life of isolation and underdeveloped potential. In fact, I believe it is one of the greatest challenges for people who either feel stuck or are too comfortable in their predictable (but underwhelming) life to make a change. Once you start taking smaller well- informed risks in daily life, it will create a positive pattern and motivate you to take chances on larger, more significant things to achieve your greatest goals. Take every risk and drop every fear because we only regret the chances we don't take. A story based on this- A man noticed a butterfly coming out of the cocoon but the butterfly was doing a lot of hardwork. Man didn't have knowledge so he actually pulled the butterfly from it's wings and unfortunately, butterfly took it's last breath. Hence, if man had let butterfly do the hardwork, it would have been alive today. Business leaders recognise this, accept risk as a cost of opportunity, and then validate this attitude within their organisations. This helps greatly in realising their goals and achieving success. Since most people tend to avoid risk, those who are brave enough to take risks already have a competitive advantage. Sometimes you need to give something to achieve something and that's also what we refer to risking.

Comparison

'The reason why we struggle with insecurity is because we compare are behind the scenes with everyone else's highlight reel' — Steven Furtick

If you compare your professional path with someone else's, it will have no positive impact on your life. Reality shows success varies depending on everyone's individual journey. The comparison will often be negative because there will always be someone better than you. Sometimes we can also refer this as perfectionism as you want to be perfect like no other. This can lead to loss of identity. We often fill ourselves so much with the ideas of others that we start to lose sight of our own ideas and identity. This can be really dangerous. You must stay true to who you are and the ideas you have. You must work in a way that suits you and your style. Research has found that comparing breeds feelings of envy, low-self confidence, and depression, as well as compromises our ability to trust others. While downward comparison, comparing ourselves to those less fortunate, can provide some benefit to one's sense of self, even this form of comparison comes at a price. It's almost like the rule of 'Having Unlike Thoughts'. Let's have a story: Kareena wants to become a nurse whereas Samaira wants to become a soldier. Kareena compares herself with Samaira. Now here the logic to perceive is that both the professions of health care and life care are equally important.

Living in the Past

'The past is behind, learn from it. The future is ahead, prepare for it. The present is here, live it' — Thomas S. Monson

First let's have a story. Niyati was very rich a year ago but due to a pandemic she faced many difficulties as her business was at downfall. Instead of working on it further, she lived in past on always thought that she was very rich before. If she would had worked harder, she must had experienced rise in her business. This is what living in past is. Focusing too much on the past can keep us permanently stuck there. Rather than spending too much time replaying how things ought to have gone, it's much more fruitful to give our past over to God and allow Him to transform our present. When you live in past, you can't work on your goals at present which will result in failure. Living in past builds loose sight of present and prevents you from a well future. Living in the past can be a difficult temptation to overcome, particularly if there are hurts and wounds that still require healing. But even if you have a complicated past that is difficult to forget, you are only borrowing time from yourself when you choose to take up residence in old hardships. Having long-term plans can also help you to be successful but living in the past makes you avoid to have long-term plans.

Caring About Other's Opinions

'Care about what other people think, you'll always be their prisoner' — Lao Tzu

It's totally acceptable when you take other's opinions or reviews but getting obsessed with them that leads to your though loss isn't acceptable. It can inhibit you from living your life, because your entire being (your personality, your thoughts, your actions) are controlled by an idealized standard of what people want to see. When you become so obsessed with other people's opinion of you, you forget your own. You become more bold and brave when you care less about what others think of you. You truly start embracing your true self and never feel ashamed of your choices in life. Others opinion stops bothering you and it is a good call. Whatever you do, it will seem bad to some and good to some as everybody as their own thinking but don't let others thinking to control your life. Everyone to mind their own business. People are entitled to think whatever they want, just as you are entitled to think what you want. What people think of you cannot change who you are or what you are worth, unless you allow them to. This is your life to live. At the end of the day you are the only person who needs to approve of your own choices. Nobody will ever be as invested in your life as you. Only you know what is best for you, and that entails learning from your own choices. The only way you will ever truly learn is through making your own decisions, taking full responsibility for them, and that way if you do fail, at least you can learn from it wholeheartedly, as opposed to blaming somebody else. A story based on this: There was a painter named Jack. He had a creative thought of placing is painting on the road side and he actually implemented it. He wrote that if anyone finds a mistake here so circle it. Later evening, when he saw his painting it was full of circles and he got upset. His friend came to him and asked him the reason he is upset. Jack briefed him everything and his friend advised him with a great strategy to make Jack learn that he don't have to care about other's thoughts. His friend told him that instead of writing if anyone finds a mistake here so circle it, write if anyone finds a mistake here so correct it. Later evening when he checked the painting, it was very clean and nothing was corrected in it

Having short term mindset

'Think long term, execute short term, experience now' — The Stoic
Emperor

Short-term thinkers focus on the now, with little regard for the future.
They make decisions and take action accordingly. Not thinking of the
future can also lead to failure. Mind-sets matter because they shape the
way we view the world and can constrict or expand the way in which we
engage in life. Our mind-sets grow out of the experiences we have.
Irrespective of whether the experience is positive or negative, a filter is
formed that limits what our mind absorbs of subsequent situations. Future
planning are always highly recommended followed by to fulfil your goals.
Think as long as you can. Let's have a story! Raima was 10-year old and she
had big dreams of achieving big. For her it doesn't mattered at all whether
she achieves something immense now or at the age of 60, 70, 80.... Raima
had planned what to do since she was 12 years old. She planned to invent
an AI Robot. Guess what? After 61 years, when she was 73, she finally
invented it and achieved her goal. This was a valuable achievement due to
which she too got certain awards. This was not only because of long-term
mind-set, it was also because of her dedication towards the goal.

Wondering the Magic

'Self believe and hard work will always earn you success' — Virat Kohli

It's some people's habit to believe on some magic and luck. They believe that god will come here on Earth, walk to their home, knock their door and serve them their dream in trays. Stop thinking like a 5-year old kid. Indeed, this can happen but only in dreams or fictional stories, not in the real world. If you want to achieve something, you are the one to work hard for that. When you 'Wonder the magic', you lost yourself into another world even if you know from inside that it's not going to happen in any way. Some people only believe in luck. They pray to god and again think that the luck (basically achievement, what people refer to) would be handful given by god. Indeed, luck can help you but will not do your work. Let's have a story: Jaya always used to believe in luck and all the time she used to sit in front of god doing no work. She also left her job. She was craving for food after a few days. All the savings went off. Instead of praying all time (though, we should pray but also work), if she would had done even a little work, atleast she would have been earning a living for herself. Working hard would result better for her life only.

Multi-Tasking

'Multi tasking is worse than a-task-a-day'

Most people refer Multi-tasking with a positive impact. But think about it that when you do Multi-tasking it stress your brain as your brain has to focus on multiple things together which is why your brain is not able to give full attention to one task and you aren't getting successful. It can hinder your performance. when the stakes are higher and the tasks are more complex, trying to multitask can negatively impact our lives – or even be dangerous. Highly successful people attribute success to the ability to focus on one specialized activity . They don't rapidly switch around from one interest to another. They start a task and then they reliably follow through with it. Whenever you focus on one task separately, it will give you better results than multi-tasking. A story based on multi-tasking- Laura always used think that multi-tasking can help her become successful. She was preparing for NEET then her mind had a sudden shot of thought of doing multi-tasking. She side by side started preparing for JEE and UPSC as well. This lead as a unknown distraction for her. Later on while giving the exams, she got entangled by what she studied for JEE, NEET or UPSC. If she would had focused on one exam, suppose NEET, so she might had clear it as she would only have studied for one exam which would not entangled her. Therefore, it's always better to focus on one task at a time.

Saying yes to everything

'Everything can't be acceptable always'

Indeed, saying 'Yes' can definitely help you many times but it can be one of the reasons of not being successful if you don't use 'Yes' wisely. Always saying yes can also leave you exhausted, stressed, and time-poor, wondering why you've been busy but not productive. Billionaire Warren Buffett, the chairman and CEO of Berkshire Hathaway, has a theory on this subject worth exploring: "The difference between successful people and really successful people," he says, "is that really successful people say no to almost everything." Notice that Buffett said almost everything. What he is speaking to is our ability to master decision-making and time management. He says we must choose, with intention, what we say yes to and what we say no to. It all comes down to simplifying, prioritizing, and focusing our attention on what matters most. Let's have a story: Aura was an artist. A day came when she had almost 50+ projects but the issue was that she had very less time to complete them. She got into this problematic situation as she accepted all the projects and not even rejected a single one. As she was not able to work on even a single project, she was never given any project again. So you see, just because of saying 'Yes' to everything destroyed her career. Hence, Somethings also have to be rejected some day.

Need of Motivation

'Success is not final, failure is not fatal, it is the courage to continue that counts' — Winston Churchill

Motivation influences our needs, desires and actions. It exists on a spectrum from zero interest to an off-the-charts drive to take action. And it often comes naturally. After all, no one needs an extra nudge to flee a burning building. In lower-stakes scenarios, though, procrastination can take over. Should you initiate that tough conversation or hope things blow over in time? What about hitting the gym now versus starting your new wellness program next week? Success doesn't necessarily require motivation or ironclad willpower. And you don't need to wake up before sunrise to drink bulletproof coffee, meditate, journal or do headstands before you can bring great ideas to life. Creating systems and habits can remove a fickle internal drive from the equation. When routines do the heavy lifting, it doesn't matter if you feel like tackling a task. You simply need to show up and follow through. Established, efficient processes will not only benefit your business but enhance personal and team productivity. Nothing will motivate you better than a fuming rage deep inside you. Focus and motivation are remarkably connected. Imagine you have three business priorities this year: expanding your team, developing a social-media marketing strategy and overhauling an important product feature. These priorities should inform everything else you do. If a project or opportunity doesn't match one of these goals, it hits the chopping block. Distractions will slip away and you'll be better equipped to make meaningful progress.

Seeking Validations

'The only approval you need in life, is that of your positive inner-self' — Edmond Mbiaka

Wondering for appreciation only? You would definitely be praised but only if you work. need for in-person validation, can create anxiety, depression, and low self-esteem, and make it addictive to hear praise, acceptance, and acknowledgment in all aspects of life. If you become an approval-seeking person, this can make a big barrier for your success. Not being able to confront people or disagree, changing your thoughts and beliefs because someone else either approves or disapproves, and ascribing your self-worth to the approval of others — all are examples of a reliance on external validation. If our life plans or even just short-term goals are guided by external criteria...without a true understanding of what it is that we actually want or what fulfils and satisfies us, then we end up at minimum disconcerted and unhappy, and at worst, with a midlife crisis or severely depressed. If in case, you don't get approved or acknowledged, it will leave you hopeless and de-motivated. You should always self-validate. But how? First and the most important step is to know yourself. What drives you? What are your values? Not your mentor's, not your boss', not your parents'. Yours. I think a lot of people, when they think about external validation, it comes in really general, broad terms. You might get anxious after submitting a big project at school or work, obsessively refreshing your email and imagining what sort of critique you'll receive. Or you might dwell endlessly on a mistake you made. But these reactions are based on emotions, the deep emotional associations in that situation that are being brought up, which are never logical. A visualization practice to help you strip the emotion from the situation in which you are seeking validation in order to see it logically.

Being honest to yourself

'Nothing makes you more vulnerable than your refusal to be honest with yourself' — Charly Emery

When you are not honest to yourself, you mostly disregard or ignore the path of success. You can justify to the world why you did what you did, but as long you are not honest with yourself, it can be difficult to find peace. For example, an individual might treat someone unfairly to gain something that was not rightfully theirs in order to be looked well upon by others. Being true to yourself is very essential as it will help you gain to count your mistakes and work upon them. You can be honest with the world, but as long as you are not honest with yourself, you are not being fair. Give the most importance to what you think of yourself rather than what others think of you. You can justify to the world why you did what you did, but as long you are not honest with yourself, it can be difficult to find peace. For example, an individual might treat someone unfairly to gain something that was not rightfully theirs in order to be looked well upon by others. But deep down, the person may know what they did was wrong. If we can't gather up the courage to be honest with ourselves, we may continue to exhibit the same behaviours. Self-honesty is a trait that holds immense importance.

A dose of over-working

'The perils of overwork are slight compared with the dangers of inactivity'
— Thomas A. Edison

Overworking can have woeful effect on your health and career. Overworking can be shown in your physical and mental health. So, if you feel something is off, it is important to listen to your body and take care of it. Overwork can even lead to serious issues like heart disease and contribute to behaviours like alcoholism due to increased stress. Your brain power get diminished ones you start overworking and as a result it can't work precisely. This can result to failure. Thus, overworked employees may simply be substantially less productive at all hours of the work day, enough so that their average productivity decreases to the extent the additional hours they are working provide no benefit (and, in fact, are detrimental). Overworking may finish your work faster but it will be less productive with less efforts of your brain. It's just like keeping a book in hand and sleeping. Researchers have found that overworking yourself can lead to more mistakes. The stress and exhaustion caused by a packed schedule can make it even harder for someone to do their day-to-day work. In fact, an overworked schedule dramatically lowers the quality of work that can be produced. We need time off, and we need to schedule the flow of work with those elements in mind.

Not using smart techniques

'Be as smart as you can, but remember that it is always better to be wise than smart' — Alan Alda

Whatever you have read till now are the basic techniques to be successful. Till the time you don't be smart, you can't achieve. Here is a technique I brought for you! It's the SCAMPER technique.

· S: **Substitute** something

· C: **Combine** it with something else

· A: **Adapt** something to it

· M: **Modify** or **Magnify** it

· P: **Put it** to some different use

· E: **Eliminate** something

· R: **Reverse** engineer it

Some more ways are:

▪ Feed your head with a variety of information as a base before you can generate ideas. As Gore Vidal puts it, "The brain that doesn't feed itself eats itself." Study a variety of literature, read biographies, read books on subjects other than yours to feed your head with enough information to let ideas germinate and flourish in your brain thereafter.

▪ Use Idea Fusion: There are no new ideas, and often, most of the ideas are just a better combination or a useful improvement over the previous inventions. After you have fed your head with tons of ideas, it's the time to put all those ideas together. Mind mapping is a good technique that you can use to make all your different ideas come out on paper, so you can make better fusion of the ideas.

Laziness- A Blessing in Disguise

'Know the true value of time; snatch, seize, and enjoy every moment of it'
— Philip Stanhope

Most people think that being lazy is bad. What do you think? Ok, hang on for a moment! Let's start with the lens of objectivity! Let's remove the wrong connotation attached to the word "lazy". Let's look at this term 'lazy' from the perspective of one of the most successful and richest people on the Planet.
"I choose a lazy person to do a hard job. Because a lazy person will find an easy way to do it." ~ Bill Gates

Sounds shocking but seems truth, doesn't it Those who don't want to work harder, find out the ways to work smarter. But what do you think? Makes sense? But Bill Gates was not the only one who had this perspective. Let's look at another figure from history. One German General named Kurt Von Hammerstein-Equord, was famous for using this principle. In fact, he used a specific categorization to assess what kind of people deserve to become highly successful in military forces. He used the following criterion while selecting his officers in his army. Here is what he stated: "I divide my officers into four groups. There are clever, diligent, stupid, and lazy officers." Usually, any two characteristics are combined.

1. Some are clever and diligent — their place is the General Staff.

2. The next lot are stupid and lazy — they make up 90 percent of every army and are suited to routine duties.

3. One must beware of anyone who is stupid and diligent — he must not be entrusted with any responsibility because he will always cause only mischief.

4. Anyone who is both clever and lazy is qualified for the highest leadership duties, because he possesses the intellectual clarity and the composure necessary for difficult decisions.

Now you would agree that being lazy is not a bad thing.

But you need to endeavour to become clever alongside being lazy to get the maximum out of your life.

Money, Money and only Money

'The goal isn't more money, the goal is living your life on your own terms'
— Cheris Brogan

Many people choose their jobs/business depending on the earnings/ salaries. Money is not everything. Ones you start working, you'll get promotions depending on your work which will automatically increase your salary. Yes, money is important and to some degree you need to factor it in but it's not the reason and can't be the focus. If you focus on money as the reason or why or as a key indicator for decisions, you'll often fail or derail the company. There has to be a stronger purpose or why that anchors what your doing or is the beacon that everything is connected to. If money is the only factor, when you hit bumps in the road (and you will) money often is not a strong enough motivator to keep you focused and persisting through. So people throw in the towel because it's a weak "why". It's also a terrible thing to base big decisions on. Any decision based off money alone is usually a poor one. Being focused on something actually important, a purpose, a why, a true solution, a vision that's connected to the company, it's products and your personal conviction is a much better focus that can stand the tests of time and that you and everyone else can get behind. While money is a thing that most people want, it's truly only a by-product of some other driving purpose that when pursued and executed on, resulted in money. So focus on something greater. Bigger than money that's actually worth pursuing and that's actually meaningful and that you love or would do for free and more often than not, that's the thing that will be easiest to make money with. Solve a real problem or follow a pure purpose and then focus and hustle doing that. Money will come.

Hobby of Excusing

'If it is important to you, you'll find a way. If not, you'll find an excuse' —
Daniel Decker

Excusing can never make you successful. It has a direct relation with procrastination. Successful people know that they are responsible for their life, no matter their starting point, weaknesses, and past failures. Realizing that you are responsible for what happens next in your life is both frightening and exciting. And when you do, that becomes the only way you can become successful, because excuses limit and prevent us from growing personally and professionally. Own your life; no one else will. It's like you are directly saying 'No' and showing your straight palm to your success. When ever you make an excuse, that makes a step ahead towards failure. Let's have a story: Anna used to work as an engineer. She always used to get late for her work and she had one excuse 'Traffic Jam', even if the road was clear. She missed a lot of things because of indirect procrastination. Due to this, it leaded to failure in the biggest project of her life. We all must have faced this situation of being late and then giving excuses, instead we shall accept the mistake and then always be punctual.

Believing on the Magic Bullet

'Every day, in every way, I'm getting better and better' —Émile Coué

Overnight success is a myth. Successful people know that making small continual improvement every day will be compounded over time, and give them desired results. That is why you should plan for the future, but focus on the day that's ahead of you, and improve just 1% every day. It's a saying that society loves to throw around whenever someone seems to rise to the top suddenly. The truth is, though, that being an overnight success is just a carefully crafted narrative. In essence, overnight success does not exist. At the very least, it is statistically so rare that people would have a better chance at "succeeding" by playing the lottery. What most people call 'Overnight success' is actually the market realising the value of a great product. But the product they realise about, it has a company, which might have took long to be successful. There is a difference between overnight success and early success. People tend to mistake the success of young entrepreneurs for sudden success. If you are an adult with a spouse, children, a mortgage and a heavy Excel workbook to make sense of it all, you may find counterintuitive, and maybe even unfair, that someone else can become a millionaire at age 19, 21 or 25. However, there is usually a story of hard work, creativity, genius and good opportunities behind such stories. People like Mark Zuckerberg, founder of Facebook, or Justin Bieber, pop music icon, did not become successful overnight. They dedicated years to learning and perfecting their craft, during which they experienced disappointment, reinvention and, finally, success. Indeed, they did not endure the decades of trial and error most of us have; yet that does not mean their success was void of effort, disappointment, struggle and the like. In conclusion, the idea of overnight success is, by all means, a misconception. Planning one's life around it is plain senseless.

Not Exploring

'Every day, in every way, I'm getting better and better' —Émile Coué

Overnight success is a myth. Successful people know that making small continual improvement every day will be compounded over time, and give them desired results. That is why you should plan for the future, but focus on the day that's ahead of you, and improve just 1% every day. It's a saying that society loves to throw around whenever someone seems to rise to the top suddenly. The truth is, though, that being an overnight success is just a carefully crafted narrative. In essence, overnight success does not exist. At the very least, it is statistically so rare that people would have a better chance at "succeeding" by playing the lottery. What most people call 'Overnight success' is actually the market realising the value of a great product. But the product they realise about, it has a company, which might have took long to be successful. There is a difference between overnight success and early success. People tend to mistake the success of young entrepreneurs for sudden success. If you are an adult with a spouse, children, a mortgage and a heavy Excel workbook to make sense of it all, you may find counterintuitive, and maybe even unfair, that someone else can become a millionaire at age 19, 21 or 25. However, there is usually a story of hard work, creativity, genius and good opportunities behind such stories. People like Mark Zuckerberg, founder of Facebook, or Justin Bieber, pop music icon, did not become successful overnight. They dedicated years to learning and perfecting their craft, during which they experienced disappointment, reinvention and, finally, success. Indeed, they did not endure the decades of trial and error most of us have; yet that does not mean their success was void of effort, disappointment, struggle and the like. In conclusion, the idea of overnight success is, by all means, a misconception. Planning one's life around it is plain senseless.

TWO

WEALTHY/RICH

We just read about how to become successful, right? What next does a person dreams? What about you? Don't you dream to be rich as Elon Musk, Bill Gates or Jeff Bezos? You do, right?

But what are the errors that cease us to be rich? Do they have any solution?

Viewing these many questions may view as normal but when you think about them, it creates as huge as an elephant list! Let's have the answers to all the questions given above!

Here are a few moves that acts as a barrier for you to become rich:-

Failing to stick to a budget

"Money is only a tool. It will take you wherever you wish, but it will not replace you as the driver." – Ayn Rand

Failing to stick to a budget can cause severe consequences for your future. In short, the most common consequences of not budgeting include a lack of savings, less financial security, out of control spending, a higher likelihood of going into debt, and more financial stress A budget helps create financial stability. By tracking expenses and following a plan, a budget makes it easier to pay bills on time, build an emergency fund, and save for major expenses such as a car or home. Overall, a budget puts a person on stronger financial footing for both the day-to-day and the long term. Many people try to stick to a budget but unfortunately, they face failure. So how I can help you by this situation? Go through the points given below!

Budgeting is important, but making a budget that is in sync with your financial profile, habits, and needs, is even more important. A lot of people make budgets but often fail to avail its benefits. There could be several reasons as to why one fails to reach a set target or goal despite creating a budget. It is seen more often than not, a lot of people fail to take note of the little mistakes they may make while budgeting which eventually leads to them not being able to stick to the plan.

1. Not making a realistic Budget

Having the right intent is good but having a practical intent is equally important. Wanting to be disciplined with your money should always start with taking into account your reality first. For instance, if you earn a monthly salary of INR 1 lac, you cannot save INR 80,000 each month! Therefore, for your budget to work you need to take into account not just your income but also your fixed and variable expenses. Not only that, make room for ad hoc spending too. Have a realistic budget where apart from savings, you have adequate overheads for spending as well. A good budget is, after all, about balance.

2. Not accounting for all your expenses:

This happens particularly when you are not aware of all your expenses. True, it is not possible to know the exact amount for each expenditure but it's important to have a tentative idea. Also, don't forget to account for those seemingly minuscule expenses that tend to go unnoticed. Sometimes, it is these little spends here and there that can derail a good budget. So, remember to account for all your expenses big and small.

3. Not maintaining an emergency fund

We all agree on the importance of an emergency fund when in need but not all of us act towards creating one when we should. Not having an emergency fund hampers your budget when faced with an unforeseen expense situation. This could lead you to dig into your investments or saving or worse still lead you into debt. To maintain your money discipline and also keep your peace of mind, create an emergency fund, however small it may be. This will come to your rescue when you overshoot your expenses in dire situations.

4. Not customizing your budget to your needs

There are some brilliant ways people budget their finances and have been known to achieve varied financial goals. While it is good to embrace these best practices, it is far more crucial that you customize your budget specifically to your needs and lifestyle. This is another major reason why some budgets fail; we try to adopt a successful budget without evaluating its impact on our financial profile. To ensure you have a full proof budget, you should tailor-make it to match your needs.

5. Not setting the right goals

A budget that has a practical financial goal is a budget that will work for you. Setting yourself up for unattainable targets will not only keep you from reaching your goals, but it will also deter your motivation. Keep in mind that you still need to take care of yourself and meet your present needs while you make a plan for the future. So, account for these and set yourself up for achievable targets.

6. Not rewarding yourself for your effort

And finally, anyone who puts in the effort and discipline needs to be rewarded. It is as important as creating and adhering to a budget. Not taking the time or money for well-deserved self-indulgence can leave you feeling unexcited or demotivated about your goals. While you build good habits, you also need to make sure you enjoy the process of budgeting and not miss out on giving yourself a little something once in a while. Have a provision in your budget for this as well. This way you won't feel left out nor will you go on a guilt-trip for spending on yourself.

These are some simple tips you can follow next time you create a budget. But remember to customize it to your profile and your needs. With a practical approach and a realistic goal, it won't be long before you start enjoying this process of budgeting if you don't forget to reward your efforts.

Would you like to read a story? Let's have one!

Jiya was one of the rich girls of the city. She would spend money as she is spending nk money. What does that mean? She used to spend money as the money is raining! She used to spend more and save less. One day, a pandemic striked her city because of which her business was going to sink and it sinked after a few weeks. She faced poverty and illness. As she got ill, she had no money for treatment. Jiya would have atleast saved for the emergency, because emergency never rings our phone before it comes!

Carrying too much of Debt

"Debt is like any other trap, easy enough to get into, but hard enough to get out of." – HENRY WHEELER SHAW

People can accrue debt in many ways. Some take out loans for houses, cars and school. Some overspend on restaurants or travel. Others rack up debt due to medical expenses insurance won't cover. Whatever the reason, most end up in collections the same way – an aspect of the consumer's life changed, leaving them unable to pay a bill. This fact makes debt collection one of the most unique industries around. As a collection agency, you work in a business to business model, serving the client creditors who originally helped your consumers. However, if you don't treat consumers with care while collecting the debts they owe, you're not likely to see much success. Even if you can manage your payments, having too much debt can lead to other financial problems like not being able to save money, missing bill payments, and having to borrow more money just to stay afloat. Carrying debt without a good plan to pay it off can lead to an unsustainable lifestyle. High debt leverage is less severe than bankruptcy but often a signal of impending doom. This means you have too much debt and your debt ratios show difficulty keeping up with your short-term and long-term debt obligations. This makes you susceptible to late fees, default and eventually bankruptcy. Having inefficient debt is more than likely reducing your wealth due to the associated interest and fees. In some cases, it may be worthwhile focusing on paying down this debt first – starting with your highest interest/fee debt, and progressively paying this off.

Debt can feel draining—especially if it's extensive. Many borrowers find their credit card statements intimidating and can't face looking at their loan balances. If you're at the end of your wits and you want to know how to get out of debt, go through ahead!

1. Gather Your Data

Before you do anything else, gather as much data about your finances as you can. Get copies of all three of your credit reports—TransUnion, Equifax, and Experian—and go through them with a fine-tooth comb. Take note of your credit score at each bureau.

Then, dig out the most recent statement for each of your accounts:

·Student loans
·Personal loans
·Mortgage
·Auto loan
·Credit cards
·Store cards

2. Make a Financial Inventory

Use the documents you gathered in step one to create a thorough inventory of your debts. This might feel stressful, but it's an essential part of any debt-busting action plan. Every time you list a debt, include the following information:

The creditor name Your current balance Your minimum monthly payment Your interest rate

Add up all of your debts, take a deep breath, and look at the total. Imagine how it would feel to be debt free. Then, come up with a set number of "months to freedom"—36 months, or 60 months, for example. Divide your total balance by the number of months you come up with to get a rough monthly payoff figure.

Keep in mind that interest will add to your total as the months progress. If your debt is mostly credit card based, you might be able to offset the extra APR with a 0% balance transfer offer—we'll talk about that option below.

You'll also need to calculate your take-home pay per month to determine if your goal is doable, or if you need to change your repayment period. You can use your monthly net pay to build a brand-new budget—and again, we'll go into that a little later.

3. Lower Your Interest Rates

You've probably already noticed the one hitch in our monthly payoff plan above—interest keeps accruing as you pay your debt off. The longer your planned repayment period, the more interest you'll pay. Depending on your interest rates and the amount you pay off each month, the interest you accrue could end up lengthening your repayment period substantially. The solution to this conundrum is to reduce or eliminate your interest rate.

4. Low-Interest Loans

Speak to your lender about reducing the interest rate on your existing car or personal loan. Home equity lines of credit usually have lower interest rates than regular loans, so if you own your own home, consider that option. You could also decide to refinance your home or vehicle to get a better interest rate. Consolidation loans—loans that wrap all your cards and various personal loans into one amount—could also help you save money. In addition to the potential monetary savings, one payment can be easier to track than several.

Interested for a story? Let's have one!

Rajiv had faced certain unconditional circumstances due to which he had take a few debts. He agreed to take loans on high interest rates as he had the need. Later on, he was not able to pay back that loan and was bankrupt. This was because Rajiv didn't thought that how will he pay back that loan. Thus, we conclude here that taking too much debts without being aware/ conscious mind, you'll never be rich. Instead of taking debts, try to be rich by your own.

Not Investing

To become rich, individuals need to build a comprehensive financial plan and need to learn how to invest. Once they learn to make their idle money work, they will be able to generate income to create wealth in the long run. And one of the simplest way to become rich is to invest early in life. Investing is one of the best ways to grow your wealth and one of the only ways to ensure the growth of your money beats the rate of inflation. It's not the best option for your emergency fund or short-term savings you plan to use within the next five years or so, but you should definitely invest your long-term savings if you want to become wealthy. You should transition to more conservative investments as you age because you'll have less time to make your money back following a loss before you need to draw upon those funds. But younger investors should invest more heavily in stocks. Stocks are more volatile than bonds, which scares some risk-averse investors, but they can also generate much greater returns. This is the art of asset allocation. But remember, don't invest in the field you are not known or have knowledge about because this can lead to bankruptcy as Anil Ambani. All investments carry some risk, but rather than sticking solely to conservative investments, try diversifying your portfolio instead. Spread your money among many assets and sectors so that a single poorly performing asset won't devastate your portfolio. Move your money to more stable assets, like bonds, as you age, but don't exit stocks completely. A good rule of thumb for the percentage of your portfolio that should be in stocks is 110 or 120 minus your age. We know that Rome wasn't built in a day; and that all good things take time. Today, when everything is about instant gratification, we are not programmed to think about benefits that might accrue 20 years down the line. The urgency to begin our personal investment journey is just not there. We accept that investing has the potential to improve our lives, yet a lack of basic investing awareness prevents us from appreciating how dramatic this transformation can be.

No blueprint to show us the wonders of compounding. Fear of the unknown and a seemingly treacherous road (risky equity markets) keeps us in the starting blocks. But the numero uno excuse holding us back is procrastination—something we are all familiar with and guilty of. More on that later. The journey of investing can be an emotional roller-coaster.

And what goes up and down, sideways and backwards, in loops and hoops
is the value of your money. Good luck doing nothing. When markets go up,
investors make money. And when markets go up further, we make even
more money. FOMO and collective greed can drive markets up to levels
where everyone around you to be making money hand over fist. What we
hate as humans more than anything in the world is losing money. A 5-10%
fall in market levels can be managed by one's own experience and
handholding by advisers. But one must also recognize that markets do
have free falls of over 20% every few years.

Growing complacent in your professional life

"Complacency is our worst enemy" – Mike Apicello

Before we move ahead, what's the word 'Complacency'? Complacency means when you are too satisfied from your work and has no worries about that which indirectly means being into a comfort zone.

Sometimes Complacency is not good. It can destroy or your career which may lead you to face financial issue. Here are a few points to prove my statements.

· Challenged Firm

Your comfort zone is a safe place where you can go to recharge or rebuild your energy reserves for the next big push. If you remain there for a long time, you may be blindsided by forces that are not under your control and that will derail your career. Are you in such a situation now? A comfort zone is an asset for your career. That is the space where you can operate from without stress because your skills are adequate to handle the requirements of the role. Thus, the wider and deeper your skillset, the larger is your comfort zone, which you should leverage to take on more risk and handle more shocks. Consider the telecom industry, which was once a sunrise sector, but currently undergoing consolidation in the face of multiple challenges. If you are working there, are you choosing to keep your head buried in the sand believing that your long experience in the role and sector keeps you safe and valuable or are you actively looking out for growth opportunities? Similarly, consider employees in grounded airlines. Many long-term employees continued to work in those airlines even when salaries were delayed or stopped, instead of jumping out before it was too late. Speak to professionals and friends outside your firm or industry to get a reality check on whether you are too complacent within a challenged industry or firm.

· Bad Geography

Geographical realities change. The city or country that you signed up for in pursuit of your dreams, transformed while you were chasing the next promotion or target. Today, an investment banker in London may pause and reflect before considering an attractive opportunity in Hong Kong—unlike in the past. Similarly, those with US green card dreams, currently are also considering other countries. Local political or social upheavals, climate, regulatory and legal changes and international trade pressures may have made your current city far less attractive than when you moved in. Having spent a few years or purchased a house or having started a family there, you may have never questioned the geography you are located in. A good plan is to annually revisit the seemingly permanent decisions you have made in your career or life and do a realistic cost-benefit analysis of sticking to the decision or changing it.

· Altered Customer Behaviour

You believe that you have built a phenomenal set of skills that were always considered critical both in your firm and industry and thus can afford to take it easy. Not necessarily true. Customer behaviour evolves and the strongest industry structures become irrelevant. Consider consulting firms where for ages, the "Path to Partner" was defined by deep influential relationships with a big customer or two. However, where the old customer needed consultants for data gathering followed by analysis and solution, the new customer has benefited from evolving technology which has placed big data at his fingertips and with analytical tools at his disposal. Thus, the new "Path to Partner" for you may lie in innovating and diversifying both services and clients instead of a single deep relationship. Reading, attending industry events and an active professional network can help you recognise these changes and take actions to stay relevant.

· Stake Holder Changes

Has the ownership of your firm changed? Or are you now reporting to a new boss? While you were comfortably operating in the past and were in a strong political position, don't expect the same when there is a change of leadership or ownership in the firm. The power equations and business priorities that you took for granted no longer hold true. Watch out for signals of change over the next quarter to a year. Evaluate the new reality and consider what changes you need to make to exist and thrive in the new reality. Else seek options that help you craft a new role within or outside your firm. Either way, expect to get stirred out of complacency.

· Job Market

Even while the world is grappling with economic challenges, India is facing its highest unemployment rate. What this means is that there may be lesser jobs or opportunities in the market for your experience and skills. At the same time, the queue of people who would love to replace you at your current role is getting longer every day. Simultaneously, consider latest disruptions in your industry and function caused by new technology. Each wave affects how business is done and potentially the relevance of your role. Are you operating from a misplaced sense of job security where you believe that the value you deliver justifies your current compensation? To avoid being displaced by someone who is willing to work for less or by new technology, step out of your comfort zone and seek avenues that make you more valuable for your firm as well as for the market where you will face stiffer competition.

RATIOS TO CHALLENGE YOURSELF
1. Effort to outcome
Does your job challenge you? Does it take effort to reach the outcomes you deliver? Here, effort is not the time you spend, but the additional mental bandwidth you need to bring to the table to solve problems. If you aren't aware of the extra effort, you are probably disengaged and in a comfort zone. Seek bigger goals.

2. Learning to application
Your journey from schooling till now has two parts—education and execution. You learn new skills in formal training or on the job while you apply experience and skills to deliver value. What percentage of your time is currently invested in learning? If it is less than 50%, you risk becoming

irrelevant in a disruptive world. Get learning.

3. Initiative to response

In the last week or month, what portion of your time was spent in reacting or responding to situations, triggers and projects not of your creation? What fraction of your time was spent in projects or ideas initiated by you? A high initiative to response ratio keeps you pushing the envelope in your career.

4. Insecurity to comfort

Are you afraid that you may be fi red? Are you anxious about failing in your project, losing face or damaging your reputation? If you answered "no" to these, you are too secure, and your career is stagnant. The honesty and depth of your insecurities is a close measure of the efforts you put in and the progress you make. Go figure.

5. Spikes over 12 months

What are your three major accomplishments over the last 12 months? If you are scratching your head right now, you do not have signify cant spikes to show in the recent past. That's a clear sign of operating in complacency. Imagine yourself answering this question next year and set yourself those 3-4 goals that you want to achieve by then.

Wondering the magic

"Success is often achieved by those who don't know that failure is inevitable." — Coco Chanel, fashion designer

You must have came across people teaching you 'If you do hardwork, you'll definitely be successful and rich. But is so practically in real life? Labour also does hardwork, is it easy for them to earn a bread of 2 times? I guess, maybe 'no'?!

Rather, if you want to build wealth, you need to combine hard work with sound financial behaviours like, financial planning, budgeting, avoiding debt, saving, investing, and living below your means. In fact, Edelman told Business Insider in a recent Facebook Live interview, "If all you do in life is work really hard, you're never going to get wealthy. Because it's not enough that you work hard to make money to set some of it aside." Edelman says in order to ensure future wealth, you must "equally" work smart. It would seem that the contrast between the rich and the poor is becoming more distinctive, so the logical conclusion is: hard work doesn't mean money! In a broader sense – if you enjoy good food, love yourself, buying beautiful things, travelling the world, you will get the money for it, or to be more accurate – you subconsciously attract money your way.

To understand how to create our realities, we need to realize that everything in this world is energy: money and our thoughts included.

The entire physical universe is made up of pure energy and vibration. When you have the insight to see everything as vibration, the nature of the universe is revealed to you and you are in control of your reality.

Every thought that we have about money or anything else, creates energy vibration and this energy starts to attract similar energies. Simply put – our thoughts are like magnets. That is the reason why cultivating positive thoughts are so important (think about your meditation practice).

When we send these energies to the universe, we attract other energies (things, situations, people) that harmonize with them. This is called Law of

Attraction – like attracts like.

Law of attraction is one of the most powerful forces in the universe and like gravitation, it exists whether you believe in it or not.

That means that your current financial situation is the outcome of your thoughts that you have had for the past days, months or years.

More than 100 years ago, Andrew Carnegie, one of the most powerful men at the time asked a young journalist Napoleon Hill to interview 500 richest people in order to discover and publish the formula for success.

Hill devoted 20 years to find out the secret of wealth. His work resulted in the book "Think and Grow Rich", which is still the best-selling non-fictional book in the world. The results are concluded in short: wealth is the result of thinking. It may sound harsh, but the painful truth is you have to take responsibility for your lack of money.

It's easy to blame the wealthy, government, class system, your employer etc., just to absolve yourself of responsibility. If you think that your financial situation is other people's fault, then you can't help yourself. All you can do is sit and moan. You are victimizing yourself voluntarily!

Hard work is nothing to do with wealth. People with poverty mentality can work punishing hours, but if they are sending negative thoughts and feelings about money at the same time, they won't attract it. Feelings and emotions are more powerful than physical efforts.

Also, despite our yearning for more, we have many hidden limiting beliefs about money that may be stopping money coming to us!

Over time we tend to fall into financial patterns that generate a fairly narrow range of results. We become comfortable with certain financial experiences; even if we don't like those experiences, they're familiar to us, so we gravitate back to them.

Have you ever looked at an ideal job but started to panic when you saw a huge salary? That what is should actually not happen. Was this too big?

Let's move on to another barrier!

Spending more than you earn

'A wise person may have money in his head, but not in his heart' –
Jonathan Swift

Anushree is a 25-year-old Fashion Stylist at a leading fashion magazine. She earns a competitive salary and aims to save at least 20% of her monthly salary. She recently bought a new car and is currently paying the EMIs. She also spends a part of her salary towards rental & living expenses. Apart from this, Anushree loves to shop, often indulging in shopping sprees. She also enjoys a vibrant social life. However, at the end of the month, Anushree often finds herself struggling for liquidity and can hardly save any portion of her income. Sounds familiar? I am sure that just like Anushree, at some point, all of us have struggled with the "month-end" blues, where our bank accounts don't necessarily agree with us. We live in the age of unprecedented opportunities and income levels. With the rise in the average income level, there has been a concurrent change in lifestyle. We also have more ways than ever before to consume and spend and this is something that is just going to continue happening. Do you think if you spend more than your earnings, you'll be wealthy? Obvious answer is no! Often, we give in to the impulse of buying something without giving any consideration to what impact it might have on our financial lives. "I enjoy each day to the fullest" or "Planning ahead is not my style" might sound very cool, but it represents a rather foolhardy thought process and can prove to be detrimental to your financial health. Extravagant expenses, no thought for future needs and absolutely no financial planning leads people to towards bankruptcy. Thus, making it more important than ever to follow one basic financial rule: "PLAN YOUR FINANCES". With this rule always in sight, it is easier to save and grow the money you earn, without sacrificing the good life.

So how do you tackle these blues? Does the battle against this "month-end" peril include compromising your current lifestyle?

Usually, you would follow the habit of first meeting all our fixed and variable expenses and then save what is left at the end of the month. This is called Maintaining an expenses budget. However, we recommend an alternate route – Maintaining a savings budget. The reason this works is that while an expense budget might help curb purchases in the short run, but in the long run, it's very difficult to be disciplined enough to stick to an expense budget. The idea with a savings budget is to set aside 15-25% of your income. This money should be deployed productively in investments, whether cash, debt, equity, or real estate. Therefore, you will have only 75% -85% of your income for your expenses. Out of this, first, you should pay off your fixed expenses such as EMIs, Insurance Premium, Rent and so on. Post that, the balance income can be used for other purposes such as shopping, entertainment, etc.

You don't need to earn in crores to end up as a millionaire. Diligent savings and planned investments will get you there too. If you follow this plan consistently, you will surely end up saving and growing your money. This is the principle of "Pay Yourself First".

Saving and investing money is as important as making money. What you do with your income today determines what you can do with it tomorrow, whether it goes up or down. It's just not productive to think, "I'll definitely start saving when I make more money" or "I don't make enough to save, so I should first concentrate on increasing my income". Instead, focus on saving, even if the amount seems minuscule. In the future, every rupee will add up to ensure a secure future. So, it's best to start as early as possible because there's no wrong time to do the right thing.

Spending more than you earn may take you to a point where you will have no money! So remove this barrier by improving yourself. Sooner or later, your hole-digging spending habits will catch up with you. Soon, you'll deplete your savings, max out your credit cards, and run out of places to borrow money. Keep your spending within your monthly income so that you're living within your means and not creating debt.

Relying on one income stream

'If you don't find a way to make money while you sleep, you'll work till you die' – Warren Buffet

Let's imagine that due to certain circumstances you get fired from your job / your business goes into loss. What will you do in this case? Will you able to live a comfortable life? Won't you face financial crisis? Of course, you will. This is because you rely on one income stream. Now, just imagine the same situation with a twist. Ones you get fired from the job or you face loss in your business BUT, BUT, BUT, you have another job with you/ or have another business which can atleast earn you a living, will you still face 'Financial Crises'? Maybe not. Because you are still earning. Atleast, from that earnings, you will not suffer. This is what the barrier 'Relying on one income stream' wants to explain you. This barrier is the one which 50% or more of the world is suffering from. This doesn't mean multi-tasking actually. This means, for example, you're doing a business/job of dresses and suddenly, due to certain circumstances it sinks but as your talent you have a melodious voice. You can go onto some stages to perform and earn a living. Diversifying income streams is a strategy the wealthiest already employ: Almost two-thirds of self-made millionaires, 65%, have at least three sources of income, according to "Rich Habits" author Tom Corley, who studied the habits of 233 millionaires, including 177 self-made. About 3 in 10 had five or more streams of income. Remember 'The more you do, the more you earn'. If you have multiple income streams, it can boost your future as even you 1st businesses/job is running well and good, but still you'll earn more profit from the another one. Adding another source of income doesn't mean "you have to think of yourself as a CEO". There are two broad categories of income: active and passive. With active income, you're earning money in exchange for performing a service. Passive income requires little-to-no-effort to make. Income stream possibilities include:

1. Salaries and wages.

You're already diversifying income streams if both you and your spouse have full- or part-time jobs pulling in a regular pay check. About 7.8% of employed individuals hold multiple jobs, based on the most recent Census data from 2018.

2. Side hustles and businesses.

There are endless opportunities here depending on the time and skills you're working with, from answering questions online to delivering groceries. You could pick one, or more: A person should pick up more than a dozen side hustles that collectively bring in $1,000 to $2,000 per month.

3. Investments and savings.

Putting your money to work in the stock market is a tried and true way to grow long-term wealth. Income streams from your portfolio might include dividends, interest from sources such as savings accounts and bonds, and capital gains. Another investment that can act as a source of income is real estate. And that doesn't always mean you have to buy an entire property to rent out.

4. Royalties.

If you write a book or teach an online class, for example, you could pull in royalty income every time someone purchases that product. That's something A person only had to create one time and now it continues to make me money.

There is enough statistics to show that families that live totally on a single source of income are at the greatest risk of poverty. Your salary shouldn't be your only source of income. Complementing your main salary is one of the most sustainable ways of buoying up your financial baseline. And thus, never depend on one stream of income.

Impulsive Emotional Decisions

When successful people find themselves in situations where they're extremely angry, sad or frustrated, they let themselves ride out those emotions without acting on them. The simple act of waiting to make a decision until you've returned to a level-headed state can play a huge role in the success you achieve. A majority, or 58%, of investor respondents agreed their portfolio performs better when emotions are left out of the equation. Yet 47% said it was difficult to keep emotions at bay, the survey found. The result is buying, or selling, remorse: Two-thirds of the respondents reported regretting impulsive or emotionally charged investment decisions. Those most likely to make those regretful moves are Gen Zers (85%) and millennials (73%). Because they have less experience in the market, younger investors may not know how to make decisions. On top of that, it's easier now to get into the stock market due to the different trading apps available. Combine that with the rise in social media investing advice, and it could be a recipe for disaster. The environment has made it easier for them to make the mistakes. Before you beat yourself up, know that it is human nature to be emotional — and trying to block your emotions is futile. Instead of trying to deny the existence of the emotion or suppress it, be honest with yourself about what that emotion that has bubbled up to the surface. Sometimes, in emotions we can take wrong decisions. Once you acknowledge it, whether it is fear, greed or something else, figure out why you are feeling this way. Then work out the next action to take based on a system you should already have in place, which addresses the companies you want to buy, how you evaluate them and when to sell or buy. Far too many people are just measuring whether they should buy or sell something just based on the movement of the stock prices that has nothing to do necessarily with the performance of the company. Instead, look beyond the daily stock price or quarterly movement to determine when you are going to sell. While people can't escape being emotional, they can choose whether or not to be impulsive. In addition to going back to your system when faced with the desire to make an impulsive decision, also take a look at the overall impulsiveness in your life. See what the triggers were for that emotion to help you identify patterns and allow you to put up some barriers. It's also important to know whether you are investing, which means holding assets to accumulate wealth for the long term, or trading, which involves frequent buying and selling. Part of the challenge is people are playing the market and they are not sure what their role is. That is why they are making these impulsive decisions. The most important emotions in relation to money are fear, guilt, shame and envy. It's worth spending some effort to become aware of the emotions that are especially tied to money for you because, without awareness, they will tend to override rational thinking and drive your actions. Intense emotions can lead to rash decisions, and anger and embarrassment may make you particularly vulnerable to high-risk, low-payoff choices. Researchers suspect intense uncomfortable emotions impair self-regulation skills. Visceral emotions can have a significant effect on decision-making behaviour. They can cause people to act against their self-interest with full knowledge they are doing so, and they can over-ride our cognition and thought processes. The psychology of money is the study of our behaviour with money. Success with money isn't about knowledge, IQ or how good you are at math. It's about behaviour, and everyone is prone to certain behaviours over other others and so are people for emotions. And thus, this barrier should be treated. Apart from this, Emotional stress, like that from blocked emotions, has not only been linked to mental ills, but also to physical problems like heart disease, intestinal problems, headaches, insomnia and autoimmune disorders. Most people are ruled by their emotions without any awareness that this is happening. We're adept at abdicating responsibility, ignoring reality, blaming others, or outsourcing the suffering to someone else. Emotions tend to drive our decisions, whether or not we acknowledge them. Fear, anger, and shame are some of the most common emotional reactions we experience.

1. Fear convinces us to confine the world to "us versus them" and "good versus evil."

· Anger says something is wrong and it must be changed — now. And of course, it's the other person who's wrong, not me.

· Shame convinces us to diminish the real concerns of others and ostracize them for thinking or acting differently. (Oppositional dualistic thinking is the human default.)

None of those sound like a wholehearted, mindfully engaged way to live.

We either learn to transform our pain or we transfer it to others. How can you be responsible with your emotions so you don't internalize that emotional harm or transfer it to others? Here's what won't help:

Why Terrified People Make Terrible Decisions

Emotions are directly tied to our sense of control. People who've worked to build a life of inner stability and peace sometimes refer to giving up control or feeling their emotions then letting them go. When we're driven by emotions only, it's an unpredictable and often disastrous ride. "Terror and fear make you irresponsible. They make you not think very clearly, right? And they make you willing to do almost anything to get rid of that awful feeling." How far do people go when they haven't dealt with the source of that awful feeling? Fear is powerful, so people who use fear can easily manipulate others. How can we break the cycle? "One of the very most powerful ways to not end up being controlled by that is to remain more curious than you are afraid. Any time in the community that there's anybody who's keeping their head, I think it's a benefit to everyone around them. I think everything is contagious. Our fear is contagious, but our courage also is. And our courage makes other people be able to be more brave, and come out of their houses, and come out of their shells, and out of their fear."

You Can't Control Your Emotions, But You Can Control Your Response

Fear, anger, and shame are easy reactions. It's easy for others to respond likewise. Emotions arise because that's how our bodies work.

It's not inherently wrong to be afraid, to wonder if there's something wrong with you, or to get angry. What matters is what we do with those signals from our bodies:

· How will we respond?

· Do those emotions have the final word, or do we channel them into something more constructive?

· Do we measure them up against the reality of the situation?

· Do we let others speak to the credibility of those emotions, or maybe how we're partly responsible sometimes?

Reframing Emotions, Not Ignoring Them

Like we avoid suffering, we sometimes avoid our real emotions because of what they're saying to us: something drastically needs attention. Instead of ignoring those emotions, blaming others, repressing our feelings, whitewashing our painful memories and the emotional baggage that comes with them, we can address things in a new way. We keep chasing those same feelings even if they're remnants of the past. Those tastes of glory keep us going back to the same sources of affirmation, or the memories of pain keep us locked up and guarded against people who remind us of someone who hurt us earlier in life. When we operate out of those emotions, we lose touch with our present ones. We trade the past we cannot change for the present we can, but we end up losing out on both if we don't snap back to reality. We can keep returning to those emotions and memories, but reframe them to help us make progress: they don't control or define us, but they were simply part of our life at that time. We're on a new path now, moving forward, making better decisions, rolling with the punches, learning to grow in a life full of variables. What does it look like for us to be brave and curious when we'd normally resort to fear, anger, or shame?

Being a control freak

Our attention spans and will power are finite. So, if you attempt to micromanage every single aspect of your life, which plenty of motivated people do, you'll end up limiting the attention you can pay to the important stuff. This isn't an excuse to do sloppy work, but you must only direct your efforts towards things you can control. For instance, if you're leaving your comfort zone and learning a new skill, accept that there will be some slip-ups. Being flexible amidst adversities is a virtue you must practice to create difference in your life. Control freaks tend to have a psychological need to be in charge of things and people - even circumstances that cannot be controlled. The need for control, in extreme cases, stem from deeper psychological issues such as obsessive–compulsive disorder (OCD), anxiety disorders or personality disorders. Control freaks experience consequences, ranging from constant irritability to uncontrollable anger. In addition to wreaking havoc on your mental health, being a control freak also wastes time and energy; both of which are finite resources. Thus, this barrier deserves a big cross! If you don't accept every situation of life, it'll definitely affect in terms of being wealthier. But, this doesn't means that you accept the situation for long-term, this means accept the circumstances but work on it and transform it. Control freaks rarely know that they are one. They believe that they are helping people with their "constructive criticism" or taking over a project because "no one else will do it right." They don't see their controlling behaviours as symptoms of what's really going on--their own anxiety has run amuck.

The Blame Game

If you ask anyone with a poor mentality why they are in the situation they are in, they will probably give you excuses like: "I was born in conditions that did not allow me to advance," "the government will not let me," or "I have too many problems."

This is because it is easier to blame others for your own problems than to admit that you do not want to or make an effort to move forward. Just imagine a situation within someone is helping you by their advises and you start to prove them wrong to verify yourself right. Here, the game starts. The moment you start with this blame game, you'll not learn to correct your mistakes, either you'll start doubting others and taking out their mistakes.

Money, Money and only Money

"You aren't wealthy until you have something money can't buy." – Garth Brooks

Your ambition is poor if it is all about making money. Money is not the end; it is a means to the end. Thinking to only earn money as it can buy everything in the world can be disastrous. I of course know that money is significant to be rich but being rich doesn't only means money! Life is not all about money; it is living out on something that outlives you. The true worth of a man is not measured with money; it is measured by the object of his pursuit. John C. Maxwell said: "Most people are capable of making a living. The significant thing is making a difference." Life is about making an impact, not making an income. Former President of the United States, Barack Obama said: "Focusing your life solely on making money shows a certain poverty of ambition. It asks too little of yourself. And it will leave you unfulfilled." When the ambition of a man is chasing after money, wealth becomes elusive. Most of the richest people in the world were just trying to solve a problem and ended up becoming the richest. Mike Murdock said: "Money is the reward you get for solving someone's problem." It is fraud when you plan to get money without solving a problem. Aliko Dangote, the richest man in Africa, said: "Every morning when I wake up, I make up my mind to solve as many problems before returning home." Dangote was passionate about solving problems and undoubtedly became the richest in Africa. Bill Gates, who has remained the world's richest man for several years, is a philanthropist committed to giving 95 per cent of his fortune to charity. It is not unusual that the man noted for solving most of the software problems in the world eventually became the richest. Why am I stating too many quotes?? This is because to prove, successful people agrees to it! Money has a path; it will always flow to the direction where problems are solved. The world of today is more effective just by looking through Gates' windows. Horace Greeley said: "The darkest hour in any man's life is when he sits down to plan how to get money without earning it." The poor chase money while the rich attract money. The right way to make money is not chasing it, but attracting it. When the ambition of a man is chasing after money, wealth becomes elusive. The youths are in a mad rush for money and material possessions. The unemployment rate in the country is alarming because youths have not realised their latent potentials and the value they have to offer to the Nigerian system. To add value to our country, we must be value-oriented. You attract money by solving people's problem, meeting people's need, seizing opportunities and following through on great ideas. Chase people's needs and not money. There might not always be money to spend, but there will always be problems to solve. Stop chasing money, look for problems and solve them. The truth is: Money is just a reflection of the value you give to others. So, the more you solve problems, the more money you will make. Some people are only passionate about doing anything just to get money, while great people are passionate about adding value to people's lives for profit. The great Ralph Waldo Emerson said: "The purpose of life is not to be happy; it is to be useful." When a man pursues purpose, fulfilment is inevitable. When a man pursues money, then fulfilment will always be elusive. It is only people that are driven by purpose that will ultimately be relevant in life. The pursuit of money alone will always make you inconspicuous in the crowd. George Washington Carver said: "No individual has any right to come into the world and go out of it without leaving behind him distinct and legitimate reasons for having passed through it." The issue of young people running after money without any definite and concrete plans to add value to the world is appalling. We seriously need to re-orientate our youths on the need to have a sense of value. We need a renewed thinking approach to wealth. Wealth is not all about money; it is about adding value, solving problems and leaving the world better than we met it. Money is not everything. Myles Munroe said: "Wealth is given to fulfil purpose and divine assignment. You were not born to make a living, but to make a difference." What you drive is not as important as what is driving you. There is a form of poverty that money cannot cure. Poverty is not the state of your bank account; it is actually the state of your mind. Some people are perpetually blocked from wealth because of the way they think and the people they surround themselves with. A wealthy man understands that there are some central and critical things in life that money cannot buy. Money cannot buy manners, morals, character, common-sense, trust and integrity. Whether spiritually, mentally, materially or socially, poverty is extremely contagious, so be mindful of who you associate with, as one relationship can make you mentally poor for life. The Nigerian youth should be a solution and not a problem in the contemporary Nigeria. Let us stop the 'mad' and 'demented' rush after money, let us proffer solutions to problems and earn money legitimately and credibly. Work hard towards evolving an idea that will solve problems and not just make money the object of your pursuit. Pursue 'meaning,' value and purpose. To the Nigerian youths, I say: "We are the solution that Nigeria is waiting for." We need to all ask ourselves this question: Am I in pursuit of money or meaning?

Conclusion

All the topics that you just read, explained and represented a game- 'The Fame Name Game'! Yes! This is a game in which we all are the participants but no one has won yet! And I must say that no one will win with the mob mentality-- that's the follow up trend! What the nonsense am I talking about this all, right? But yes, this is the bitter truth of today's society! One of them what I sincerely have to mention is --- We want others to go backwards but we? We keep standing right there where we were before. Understand that you don't have to follow this follow-up trend or the mob mentality. If you would really like to have comparison with others, start with equality and then take this competition ahead. Because race takes place when both or more participants are standing at the same starting point otherwise it would be called 'partiality'! Let others come equal as you and then start the race where you have to go ahead instead of pushing someone back. So loose this tradition of pushing someone back (the mob mentality). Second thing in this 'Fame Name Game' is 'The Snap believe'! What's this? This is a believe where you think that anything you want to achieve can be achieved just in fraction of seconds! We all want to achieve everything so fast that this mentality sometimes itself pushes us back. I know, at first it sounds exciting still but in future you'll have repentance. You walk step by step, that's first step then second then third and so on. But if you decide to take 100th step right after the 2nd step then definitely you'll face very difficulties and there are certain chances to get fail. Instead I prefer to walk step by step and reach your goals smoothly. Well, these were just 2 mentalities that I explained but there are many though. All I want to conclude with is that if you are in this 'Fame Name Game' make sure that you walk alone not with the group of people with mob mentality!

www.ingramcontent.com/pod-product-compliance
Lightning Source LLC
Chambersburg PA
CBHW070843160726
48004CB00001B/480